THE DETACHABLE MAN

THE DETACHABLE MAN

POEMS BY

DONALD FINKEL

Atheneum   1984   NEW YORK

Some of these poems, or versions thereof, have previously appeared in *American Poetry Review, Antaeus, Ascent, Chicago Review, Chowder Review, Grand Street, Green River Review, Iowa Review, Jumping Pond, Kayak, Madison Review, Ontario Review, Other Islands, Perspective, Poetry Miscellany, Poetry Now, Shenandoah, Tendril* and *Space Age Review.*

"The Old Man on the Trampoline" was originally published in *The New Yorker.*

For F.P. loose at last

CONTENTS

THE DETACHABLE MAN

HOW THINGS FALL

CONCERNING THE TRANSMISSION

You might say the same of poetry:
you've sunk too much in it
to quit now, driving
good hours after bad
too much of you wound
round the wires and the hoses.

You might stop addressing
this absence beside you,
cursing through the intricate
cities, singing in the high passes,
tooling down freeways,
minding the numbers,
ears pricked for oracular
tappings, limping past fields
of sullen junkers, eyeholes crawling
with nettle and goldenrod.

If you let go now, the bearings
will scream from their orbits,
the rocker arms clang in their cylinders
and the needles return to their various zeroes,
as if your hands had never clenched
this sweaty wheel.

HITTING THE ROAD

All afternoon the death wind roars at the vents
but we keep to the right-of-way, hurtling
through a rain of locusts and green dragons
past a mole-grey mongrel, partly flayed,
or a flat black carcass where a tire has died.

Side by side we hunker in our blunder-bus.
Its wide unblinking eye's a web of thready
guts, thoraxes, pincers, wings,
egg-yellow, pomegranate, plum.
June bugs ping like bullets off its chromium grin.

Humping in our wunder-wagon, twin lobes
in a padded skull, we ride, neither kissing
nor parting. You sing me wanderlieder while
I work the pedals, Indianapolis to Wheeling.

LEAVINGS

1

Tied in her iron crib like a withered baby,
sinking through infancy as if
she would come unborn, Mother shakes
the I-V clip in her fist like a tinker toy
and thrashes at her bandages, revealing
one livid thigh. From this I came.

2

With a ghost cough and a throaty rattle,
to the twitching bluegreen star
on the monitor screen, to the gasp and sigh
of the breathing machine, her blue lips flutter,
her fitful ember breasts the dark.
Bile streams from her nostril into a beaker.
To this return.

3

Last spring she tried to leave
through the rest home window. *Some rest,* she wheezed,
and hailed a patrol car: *Take me to the Hilton, cabby.*
Leaning back, she groped for her purse
and felt her heart snap open, all but empty:
one lime life-saver, shrouded in lint,
two lichen-green pennies to rest on her eyes.

4

There's nothing left for me now but to leave.
On the way to the elevator, history
dissolves behind me down the corridor.
Old scars and trophies, relics, pride, regret:
my losses fall away from me like fruit,
sweetening the worm's hardtack and compost tea.

5

THE LADY DOWN THE STREET

cannot suffer the little children.
They scatter from her driveway shrieking,
laugh-dust in their hair.
Her husband is alive and happy in Indianapolis,
safe from the naked edge
of her affliction.

Her eyes tremble in their wells like haunted water,
calamity floods from her bloodred lips.
Her life-mask shudders and wrinkles
in the flame of her torment.
From out of disaster
she lifts an ashen arm to greet me.

Writhing, her bluewhite hair
turns my heart to stone.
I carry that home in a sack
and leave her fluttering,
a dry leaf caught in the thorns
like the ghost of a rose.

PROGERIA

The wizened nine-year-old Methuselah
playing kickball in the schoolyard
bruises easily. Besides,
his wind's not what it was, his knees
creak in his jeans as he shuffles
through second childhood long before
his first runs out.

          The date on the paper
changes as I pick it up, the planet's
spinning a little faster still. The children
know it already, the poor and the halt.
Up there the clouds are giving
the steeples suck, spurting from
dingy nipples spirits so raw
they etch the brain and scour
the senses black, the tears are coming back
with all their salt.

          Clasped in his mother's
arms he croaks, *Don't hold so tight mama
you hurt*. Strangers, it is we
who come slouching each daybreak
to bear him away, to bind him
on the stone of our compassion,
to grope in his side for the clamorous
hummingbird heart.

          Rising from his nap
he spreads his spindling arms like
April twigs to the late afternoon,
toasting with his five-oclock milk
the mothpale moon, trembling seven-fold,
fervent as a mayfly to begin the night.

IT WAS SOMEONE

It was someone she knew,
someone she trusted,
slid back the chain for,
opened her lonely door.

It was someone she didn't know,
opened his heart to her,
showed her the hunger
crouching inside,
lips drawn back
in a shamefaced grin.

Now from its staple
the chain hangs, inviolate.
The latch sleeps serenely,
its one eye open.

Thoughtless and vague on her
much-crumpled comforter,
her eyes admit
dawn and the janitor.

On her pale throat
the thumbs of hunger
have left their print.

OUR WOUNDS

The mongrel licks his thorn-torn forepaw
doggedly, a dithyramb of licking,
an epic of cleansing.
His wound glistens, naked as water,
as unashamed.

We let our wounds skin over,
a crust of desiccated gestures,
old grimaces stiffening into masks
while we look away.

Then we worry them with our thumbnails,
working relentlessly inward from the edges
till at last they bleed.

HOME REPAIR

When you come down at night from your cheerless attic,
from your day of hacking, spackling, screwing, patching,
soldering sonnets of obstinate plumbing,
two hundred twenty volt toccatas,
when you come down from sawing and scraping,
paint-flecks on your beard and glasses,
you smile at me through a splatter of offwhite stars.

Tell me, old improvisor, my left hand man,
why they call it dexterity,
that access of desperate carpentry, that orgy of craft.
And tell me, is there one tool left
in your prodigious chest to splice the girl downstairs
who rinses her hair in your basin,
strokes it in your steamy mirror? It crackles like naked wire,
brushing the stainless shoulders of disregard.

THE LEFT-HANDED JUGGLER

The left-handed juggler has everything it takes
to reel in those steak-knives whickering past his ears
except dexterity.

Rectitude, he mutters. *Righteousness. By rights.*
Kingdoms teetering on the point of a word,
sharp as a scream,

self-evident as a splinter under a thumbnail. He lets
the fearful helix snicker on. How can he be
right in the head

out there risking his earlobes and his life, and for what?
For three squares and a flop? Right now for once
he'd set things left,

but the terrible cutlery of circumstance
whirls counterclockwise round the right-of-way, caressing
his sinister fingers.

THE TRANSMUTATIONS OF AIR

Brained on my astounding windowpane
the wren sprawls in the stubble, one wing splayed,
half-risen and half-stunned.

He'd climb in tightening spirals on his one good wing,
a solar moth,
a shipwrecked sailor hauling at a single oar,

if the wind didn't bear down so implacably,
a slab of cold blue sky
smeared by a cloud no bigger than a glazier's hand.

ONE MORE SPIDER

A noiseless patient spider, I
mark'd . . .   WALT WHITMAN

Take this one, this vermilion midge
dangling from the maple,
a droplet of blood at the end of its rope,
precarious, trusting in the bright abyss,
waiting for the breeze to give her a push.

In this silence the least whisper might take her.
You can hear from here the click of her
miraculous needles, knitting a lifeline
thin as a syllogism.

Whereas patience, Walt, how too much
like a man it is, time upon time
venturing all on each cast, patient
as a worm on a hook with his life on the line.

Or follow that thread back to the intersection
where the maple reaches out one scrawny arm
sheathed in dustgreen rags, where flesh meets grass,
where one thought spinning out
meets another coming back.

Where the sutures meet, Walt,
dabble your toes in the soft
sinkhole in heaven's skull.
With your sweaty palms,
push off
and fall,
headlong
maybe but
patient
no.

A QUESTION OF MEMORY

Every morning
the doctor with rimless glances
asks her for the date.

Forgetting backward
she disremembers this morning,
then yesterday,

reels in the years,
undoing the web of her life from the outside in.
Last winter hisses behind her brow, erased.

Caught in her mouth, a memory stirs,
the husk of an enormous moth
that crumbles at the touch.

Voracious, inconsolable, she wolfs it down,
croaks at the doctor, *I know your game!*
and scowls at the wall.

Under her door she can see the days
pass in the corridor like empty wheelchairs.
An inmate shuffles past,

dragging his walker like a portable cage.

LATE FEBRUARY THAW

One night of rain,
the snowman's down
to his wet black bones.

A light wind wrings
three last bright tears
from the pin-oak tree.

By the house, a tumble
of shining ice-tiles
fallen from the eaves.

From under the bleak
Euclidean snow,
the fractal grass:

a hexagram for what,
this cloudless mild
St. Louis of the soul?

Persistence of the broken.
Perseverance furthers.
For once, no blame.

THE PERILS OF LAUGHTER

*The term cataplexy literally means "being struck down,"
and the emotion that evokes it is most frequently laughter.*

NATHANIEL KLEITMAN, *Sleep and Wakefulness*

Out here, in the doldrums,
where the treading is easy,
rising on muffled swells,
peering down the long slow troughs,
the feeblest snigger is fatal,
the least whisper of frolic.

> Some patients have time to sit or lie down on the floor
> so that they do not fall.

All at once the tendons everywhere
desert their posts, yield
in a body, leaving the bones
to fend for themselves,
the spine a string of ivory beads
in a blood pudding.

Sinews unstrung, the flesh
surrenders to the overwhelming
arms of water, even here
On the threshold of a boundless yawn.

> The patient may be able to ward off an attack of narco-
> lepsy by engaging in some form of activity; an attack of
> cataplexy, by learning to curb his mirth or, if he cannot
> suppress his sense of humor, by withdrawing from the
> company of friends.

Forsake all crowds,
all weddings, wakes,
housewarmings, balls,
all banquets, carnivals.

Laughter is endemic,
passing from mouth to mouth.

Abstain from festivals,
picnics, pow-wows and symposia,
deadly revels, rank with foul palaver,
unwholesome banter, pestilential laughter.
Keep out of poolrooms,
discotheques, cantinas.
Snickers are lethal, smiles are suicidal.

Renounce fiesta,
shun horse-play,
abandon whoopee.
Even here, far from shore,
riding these measured
solemn, reasonable swells,
I hear the thunder of multitudes,
the ominous rataplan
of cackle and guffaw.

THE LAST HOURS OF
PETRONIUS ARBITER

1

> *Within a few days there fell, one after
> another, Annaeus Mela, Gaius Ancius
> Cerealis, Rufrius Crispinus, and Petronius.*

TACITUS, Annals

If the whirlwind that struck Campania that year,
toppling villas, levelling cottages, mowing
the fields alike of merchant and aristocrat,
appeared republican to its weirdly calm
dispassionate heart, the plague that devastated
the capital was downright democratic.

> No miasma was discernible in the air. Yet the houses
> were full of corpses, and the streets of funerals. Neither
> sex nor age conferred immunity. Slave or free, all suc-
> cumbed just as suddenly.

Wives perished on their husbands' fading embers,
daughters on fathers', where two years before
the bones of Rome lay smoldering.
Nor spared that pestilence harlots or cutpurses,
centurions or senators, the great
lay down with the contemptible.

> But their deaths seemed less tragic; for by dying like
> other men they seemed to be forestalling the emperor's
> bloodthirstiness.

For Nero's reigning fear, on the other hand,
wasted only the wealthy and the well-favored,
the overly gifted and the too-much-praised.
Grimly imperial, patrician to the end,
like his appetite, the royal paranoia
silenced Piso the dissolute and Seneca the wise,

Quintianus the conspirator and innocent Silanus,
that ill-starred gentleman whose one offense
was to be noble and respectable at once.

2

> *And, you know, I once saw the Sibyl of*
> *Cumae in person. She was hanging in a bottle,*
> *and when the boys asked her, 'Sibyl, what*
> *do you want?' she said, 'I want to die.'*
>
> PETRONIUS, *Satyricon*

By Bacchus' puckered scrotum, I confess,
by Nero's tits, by the knout of Priapus,
I shrank behind a pillar, for once dumbstruck,
while those wheyfaced hooligans, in their scrofulous Greek,
like so many scraggy hatchlings, twittered and screeched
the selfsame phrase my daimon whines each dawn
when I kick my slippers off and reel to dreams,
having dipped my wick in every seething crack,
from knuckle-rumped old buggers to rosy-cunted
maids with nipples hard as babies' thumbs.

Let me come clean, old boy. I gaped like a yokel
at that withered harpy, vexed, interrogated,
shrivelled by inquisition, grilled to a scruple,
slumped like a wizened fetus in her jar,
from which her answer issued, hoarse and dry,
addressed to no one in particular,
my words, Asclytus, mark you, mine precisely:
I want I want I want to die die die.

3

Look, a little to the left, where a razor scar
leers, thin-lipped, through a gap
in the bandages, as the cadaver-jawed
pianist takes one last drag on his coffin nail,

a little to the left, where the thin haze frails
through the VA ward like a disconsolate fugue,

19

a tad to the left, the astronomer's dodge
to trap dim stars with the naked eye,

a thought to the left, where the infinite
lours through the ravelled fringe of the Milky Way,
where my own death swims from the bright abyss
like a shivering star and snags in a ragged seine

of capillaries in the corner of the eye:
one bright drop rises at the tip of Petronius'
extravagant dagger, where it intersects
the blanched campagna of his wrist.

4

*Petronius deserves a brief obituary. He spent
his days sleeping, his nights working and
enjoying himself. Others achieve fame by
energy, Petronius by laziness.*

TACITUS, *Annals*

Curator of pleasure, professor of revels,
counsellor, critic, connoisseur,
godfather Nero's contract on his head,
disdaining equally both hope and fear,
rode to his beachfront villa at Cumae and threw
his last, best festa, ortolan stuffed with fig,
and honeyed dormice rolled in poppy-seed.

He severed his own veins. Then, having them bound up
again when the fancy took him, he talked with his friends
—but not seriously, or so as to gain a name for fortitude.

Presiding at his stylish wake, he stole
the scissors of Atropos to snip his thread.
Thinned with prime Falernian, the bright blood seeped
through the bandage to the boozy strains of Nero's guard,
while outside the temple of Hercules the Sibyl
dangled deathless in her jar, while a few bored stars
peered down the alleys of Cumae, looking for a party,
and the moon lay down on the sea's cold tongue like an obol.

LATE NEWS

In the blue eye a village drowns.
A boy bursts into flame.
The cavalry mows down another field of Sioux.

How long can I sit here
parked on this sleepy shoulder,
strictly neutral,
ticking over,
thoughtless as a cat?

The eye is vacant,
blue as my own.
The hound lies whimpering under my chair.
His legs begin their slow side-stroke,
he's running in place.
All day he waits by the door
for something to chase.
He's found it now
or it's found him.

If there were nothing to fear
the flesh would invent it.

WATCHING MY STEP

If I keep my head down
I can see my feet,
stalking the snail's trail,
the highway of the ant.

If I keep my head down
the rain won't warp my glasses.

If I keep my head down
I may escape
the attentions of our friendly
neighborhood sniper.

I can hear the maple
tearing the sky into dustrags,
the aerial clawing
the sky's blue overalls.

WHAT MY HEAD IS FOR

To keep my ears from squabbling.
To pound on the door of judgment
when my knuckles are sore.

To keep my nose out of the sewer.
To hold souvenirs, old keys,
worn yellow pebbles, a parching tongue
cracked like a castoff shoe.

To lift my eyes above my appetite.
To read the writing over urinals,
peek through windows, make out scrawls
in matchbooks praising black motels
I never slept in, bearing
one last match, whose rosy head
I still may strike against the dark—

a head with a future, not like this one,
doomed never to flower on my shoulders,
destined ever to nod nod on its stalk
at the merest breath of reason,

a head that does not settle
in the cup of my palms like cloudy water,
a head I might strike
on the smog-brown backside of night
and set the blue tongues singing under my soup.

STROKING THE CAT

Just when we'd drifted off so peaceably
rising and falling on that tranquil roar,
that apotheosis of breath, your purr,
your claws begin as if of their own accord
to flex themselves in my defenseless thigh.

Even your tool is set with tiny spines.
The act begins with a groan and dies with a scream,
not shamefaced, sheepish, back-to-back like dogs,
but every-which-way, yowling to be free,
snagged on the pitiless brambles of desire.

Grown men in the performance of your rites
ofttimes transfix their innocent instruments
with fish-bones, twigs, pig-bristles, silver awns.
Nor can I bear to put you down myself,
throbbing here in my lap like an engine of pleasure.

My blind thigh twitches in sleep. This peace has thorns.

EVERY DAY IS THE FOURTH OF JULY

Under the vast marquees the solitary
sad cashiers read Kafka in their cages
by the borrowed light of starbursts,
neon and phosphor.

The Puerto Ricans are picnicking on their front stoops.
Drunks and bag ladies make speeches
on every corner.
Buses let fly chrysanthemums of smoke.

Sparklers rise from the ruddy frycook's griddle
while, behind parked Cadillacs, pubescent thieves
set off the perilous
cherry bombs of boredom.

WHY WE DIDN'T RENT THE CABIN

Because we knew not a single
flower's name, because we had nothing
to say to the tiny vermilion stars
crouching in the nameless green
tangle of weeds, because the burly
gas-cylinder hunched in the underbrush,
a stranger spying on strangers.

Because no asters raised their
customary violet constellations
to guide us to the clearing's edge,
because no columbine shook its
scarlet jester's cap-and-bells
to greet us, no jewelweed nodded
its succulent flamegold corollas.

Because through the farther trees someone
nameless, less strange perhaps than we,
hefting what could only have been
an automatic weapon, sent
round on baffling round into
the dim green side of afternoon.

Backing down the driveway spitting gravel,
trusting the blind curve and the sudden
silence, I felt a tick groping the sunless
hairs of my skin, another nomad seeking
only a quiet meal and a room for the night.

THE MAN ON THE TRAMPOLINE

The man on the trampoline
lets himself down gently
but firmly. He knows
there is a bottom to every season.
He stretches his toes to touch it,
disappearing to the waist.

The web yields,
tightening, tightening,

till he finds the nadir.
Then, toes together,
dancing on a needle,
arms lifted, as in flight,
his white robes billowing
in the sweaty, desolate gymnasium,

he rises from his tomb
toward the star-streaked skylight.

SALISBURY CATHEDRAL FROM THE BISHOP'S GROUND

Constable, 1823

If, by melting or smelting, by roasting
or blasting, solution or dissolution,
they wrought the transmutations of lead,
by precipitation, by flaking or grinding
from greasy slate to chinese scarlet,
from grizzled ash to royal red,

to what might humble lead aspire,
burning yellow, blending green,
that grey stones reach for milky clouds,
that under Salisbury's soaring towers
Constable's cows might safely graze
and meek grass turn to clotted cream?

WHEN THE LIGHTNING STRIKES

You will remember nothing.
You will remember nothing of these
millennia while your hand inexorably
closes round the glass, and your molecules
serenely rearrange themselves.

When I count three and snap, the glass
will fly into shards.
You will unfold from your chair
and slump to the floor like a wounded carp,
thrash away from the open window, leaving
a trail of blood on the carpet
which will dry by morning a poignant umber.

You will remember nothing when you wake.
You will remember wanting only not
to die, not yet,
as they lift you to your feet,
giddy, bleeding, green, original,
raging to alchemize and replicate.

HOW THINGS FALL

Dust settles. Stars decline.
Curtains plunge. Splendor sprawls.
The sleeper falls back on his dream.
Princes fall out. Troops
fall in.

Shoes fall on their feet,
angels to their knees.
The note falls due, the day
falls into place. Leaves fall
like suicides, drifting reluctantly,
whispering in the wind they make.

A pound of feathers falls
like a pound of flesh. The word
falls short. The balances tremble.
The butterfly falls to the twig
and clings, flittering.
When the temple falls
every shard's a temple.

When the city crumbles
won't the masons have their day?
A feast of heavenly mortar,
an orgy of stones.

BREATHER IN EDEN

BREATHER IN EDEN

For the chaste blue mountain air
we fled together, dodging villainous semi's,
sixteen hundred miles of implacable cactus.

Now down the Alley of the Dolorous Virgin
a lumbering dump-truck thunders over the cobbles.
The afternoon is drenched in attar of diesel.

Then a jackdaw whets his beak on the TV aerial:
a slim breeze shivers and wakes and the garden's
suddenly sweet with essence of burro dung.

The sun beams down from the blameless sky
on this sinful Eden dripping with unjust desserts.

PRIME

At dawn the bird begins to sing
who is the blind man's light,
joining the roosters and the bells.
His cry is a descending scale
of hyaline tears,
receding like laughter.

LESSON #33: LA TIA DE LA CRIADA

No le pegan más, she wailed,
stumbling over the cobbles toward
the malevolent trio flailing her son
with handtooled belts.
Don't hit him again.

Y tú, the tall one roared.
You're another, as his belt
wound round her skull like a leather
bandage, corner of the buckle last
to nail it down.

Her aunt, says the maid,
who was only yesterday stirring
the *pozole*, who was only yesterday
no one to me, is *nadie* to her,
withdrawn, beyond all palaver
as beyond pain.

For her the great bronze clappers
are muffled at last,
no le pegan más, which are for me
now barely begun.

THE MAN IN THE STREET

The man in the *salida* (that is, *way out*),
the one our downcast low-beams brush as we climb
the long, steep helix out of town
may well be dead, or dead drunk (or merely, like us,
on the way out).

       Neither of us speaks,
or looks back to see, or turns to salt
though, passing the *mirador* (the *overlook*),
we look out over the benighted mountain town
sprawling down there like a field of bedraggled stars,
each light a tiny sun around which swarm
a rabble of shadowy griefs and unspeakable fears.

TRANSACTION

For a coin of the realm
he lugs my lady's garbage
to the dump by the arches,
hugging to his scraggy breast
two great sacks bursting
with plenty, rich with grease.
Heady with oranges
and rancid meat, he marches,
beaming like a saint
in a foretaste of candy.

END OF IMPROVEMENT THANK YOU

> *El deber de poeta*
> *Consiste en superar la página en blanco.*
> *Dudo que eso sea posible.*
>
> NICANOR PARRA

And what of this page, before I loosed
my Pilot Razor Point? a snowswept mesa
vacant as an angel's mind.

And what of the perfection that distends
the nursling's all-too-spherical belly,
sucking nothing from his mother's dug
but pure transcendence?
Oh precious tablet, irremediably marred.

The painter thrusts his stiff new brush
in a glistening mound of alizarin
and faces the canvas, smooth, broad,
faultless and terrible as Athene's brow.

In the bank an old man stoops to retrieve
his crooked stick where it snoozes
on the cyanic tiles by his huaraches,
cracked, tough as ten-day-old tortillas,
interposing his body between the sleepy teller
and the timid samaritan, poised in his faultlessly
faded jeans and impeccable running shoes.

Oh for a sea unlittered with the bones of coral,
for a night without stars, or one star
trembling in the seamless indigo twilight,
for one slim possibility, skimming the mesa
before it stoops to prey.

The old man snatches up his stick
while the tourist teeters.

The famished child unsheathes
its milk-teeth, drawing blood from the nipple.
The painter slashes the immaculate canvas
opening long alizarin wounds.

And what extenuates this skewbald page?
Nothing. Nothing but the voices rising
as if other ears, as famished, as rapt,
were listening, as if
these scars were a thousand tiny mouths,
crowblack, clamorous and passionate.

BRICK-SONG

Gusts of music sweep
from the bricklayers' Philco,
wafting from its black calyx
attar of saxophone,
pheromones of guitar.

From their brick-pink roof
a hodman crows like a gamecock,
a grackle answers.
I'm laved in a sea of palaver,
birds, bells, ching ching
of trowel trimming brick.

They will make, name it,
of brick and fresh mortar,
a chimney, a chapel,
an altar, a three-storey ark
brimming with brick flamingoes
and blushing doves.

They will lay me a ceiling
flat as a mill-pond
and dare me to dance on it.

THE BLUNDER CIRCUS

El Circo Blunder rumbled in last night
and raised a mossgreen tent on the soccer field.
Three yellow semi's debouch
a trickle of wild life, offloading
elephants, ponies, peacocks, anacondas,
the clean and the not-so-clean,
a freakish ark, a convoy of arklets
tacking from peak to peak.

Now through the town
a van called *Blunder* trails a wake
of turbulent children, blaring the word.
The Six Hundred Year Old Man has set up an altar.
He's calling them round:
his wife the contortionist, the clowns his boys,
and their wives the Giantess
and the India Rubber Maid and the Tattooed Lady.

The mannerly lion strolls in with the mangy ape,
the Salamander Girl slithers hand in hand
with the Human Torch—outcasts and innocents,
an alternate seed-world, hybrid, migratory,
four hundred and fifty thousand
stupendous cubits cubed of glitter and roar:
our second chance.

MAGUEY

For nearly seven years it bristles there
shaking at the sky all twenty ineffectual spines
as if, should he make up his mind, the old man
couldn't reach right over with one remorseless limb,
lay open its belly with a flick of his sickle, and drink
the sweet white blood. For weeks they'd go on like **that,**
bristling and drinking, a needle-witted farmer
milking a fat green porcupine.

Instead, in the seventh spring, the change begins.
Sprouting from its belly, a ten-foot sapling-thick
asparagus thrusts into the astonished sky
and explodes in a thousand improbable yellow flowers
attended by bumblebees plump as hummingbirds,
hummingbirds like gigantic bees
and elegant black-and-saffron butterflies.
Then, winking in his window, the old man
will toast the multitude with Seven-Up.

COMING

Small and taut as a jockey in her whipcord jodhpurs,
the English lady ponders from her doorway
the old man plowing down by the shriveling reservoir,
trailing his cloud-white ox at the same inperturbable
shuffle as yesterday when, coming through the scrub,
glancing neither at her nor at her newly
battered lemon-yellow Rabbit, he set
one wretched huarache in front of the other, as if
down an almost discernible furrow to where
his burro languished, still as meat on the shoulder,
one fathomless brown unblinking eye agape
at the ox-white clouds grazing their vast blue pasture.

One hand on her crumpled fender, one on her heart,
she paused as the old man reached for the lead-rope,
yanked it once, twice, calling *ven, come.*
And bless her if it didn't kick out, before and behind,
then scrabble to its feet and follow the old man back
down that necessitous furrow.
                      Now's he out
by the perishing reservoir, in the wake of his ox,
plowing the fecund, lately-risen acres.
If the water won't come to him, he'll go to the water.

THE FISHERMEN

paddle from the island to greet us,
circling their haggard canoes
between our launch and the pier.

Dipping and lifting the wings
of their butterfly nets,
they dredge up shadows.

The captain passes a basket among us,
gathering pesos to pay for them.
On every knot in the mesh

tiny stars blaze in the noonday dazzle.

AT THREE A.M. THE DOGS

strike up a tune.
One sounds the downbeat:
what's he caught,
what scent, what inspiration?
The moon smells acrid as always
like cheap regret.

Others pick up the tune now,
each at his own pitch.
Some take the high notes, some the low,
bassos and coloraturas,
one heartfelt phrase, repeat ad nauseam
their dogged oratorio.

The chorus keeps it up
as stars rattle softly in the sky's black calabash.
How classical. How chaste.
To each his own appropriate refrain,
one trenchant epigram to see him through the night
like *thief!* or *don't!* or *mine! mine! mine!*

THE OTHER DOGS

Here they stalk the street
like cats, all bones and business.
Mostly they keep their teeth to themselves.

They know whence cometh
their sustenance, but
mind your shoes.

For a price, one will sit at your gate
and guard your house
from the other dogs.

ARTLESS DODGES

Sunning herself on the chapel wall
a lizard waits, a slender narcolept,
for wind to drop her
a cropful of bitter crumbs from his high table.

When I come hulking round the corner,
vast and affable as a brontosaur,
she wakes, the leathery nymph,
skittering through the bougainvillaea,

her shadow caught like an iron-grey lash in the corner of sight
while, hovering round the blooming maguey,
a hummingbird creaks at me like a tiny door.
Their airy stratagems elude my eye:

to hold my course by constant flight
and keep my hold by letting go,
eternities of tireless ardor,
diminishing intervals of repose.

IN A DRY TIME

In a dry time, Señor Lopez
spills from the cab of his rusty tanker,
grinning in a nimbus of diesel,
his generous belly oozing from his shirt.

From the back of his tanker
three green hoses snake through the doorway,
dangling their snouts in the cistern,
feeding the wizened body of our water.

Every morning we lift the lid of her coffin,
gnaw all day on her dank blue bones.
A flock of stray clouds grazes the uplands,
herded by a mangy wind.

All day the sun gleams on the parching cornfields
like a fat gold tooth in a sky-blue grin.

MORNING

Esperanza sweeps the last of last night's rain
before her, angel of daybreak, driving
the waters of darkness back with her straw sword.

ALL WE NEED

Last night at last, the first rain worth the name
stooped from the moonless sky and struck the town
like a hawk of water.
In the land where the word for affluence is *agua*,
Too Much sank its beak in Not Enough.

Between the organ cactus and the candelabra,
up to his ankles in fragrant clay,
the nopal spread his hundred thumbless mittens
and presto! snatched from the torrent
clusters of succulent bluegreen flowers.

In the steep streets, cobbles climbed from their beds
and waddled toward the plaza
where, this morning, two brass bands
raise two contending halleluias,
while a drum lays down a separate beat
for the conchero-dancers.

Stripped to their breech-clouts and seashell anklets,
they are beginning the dance of All We Need.

THE DETACHABLE MAN

SAVORING THE SALT

He takes the cold way home, along the boardwalk,
in the brackish, gaunt Atlantic City dawn.
Beside him in the somnolent casinos
wheels turn dreamily on sea-green tables,
brigades of one-armed bandits hold up morning.

The sea-wind kisses him fiercely, leaving on his lips
the smack of straining rope, of creaking holds,
astringent, keen, a penny for the helmsman,
sour as recollection, shrewd as doubt,
dank as his mother's brow in the midnight ward.

To make good his losses, to replenish his waters:
his daily brine. He runs the tip of his tongue
across the knife-edge of his smile, to take it in.

SOLITAIRE

Always an empty chair:
pull up a six-pack, sit in.
The ashtray overflows,
ditto the frigidaire,
so pop a frosted can,
crack a fresh deck and begin.
Lay them each by each,
then pick them up again.
Always an ace in the hole,
always a smiling jack
to lay on the widow queen.
Always a vacant chair
across the worn green baize
to make a game of it,
and nothing but time to lose.

ELECTION DAY

Up since daybreak, he cast his worm with the earliest birds,
flew down to the grade school gym and exercised
his insufferable right to choose,
among losers, the one least likely to exceed.

One cheer for the off-white knight on the scrawny horse
and the stunted platform: *A pinch of salt in every pot.*
Asperity's around the corner.
Hole in his gauntlet, couldn't sell a Cadillac to an arab.

Mind, not that our citizen's bored.
A tang of civic fervor still kindles his blood,
but the whole bitter day's before him
and the bars are closed.

Not a twig in this twittering city
to roost on for a spell in the glow
of this uncommon communal fever
while it still simmers.

ON THE BEACH

On his perpetual expedition to the sea,
barefoot as a pilgrim, holding his shoes,
he pauses on the still-damp sand at the verge of the tide,
watching the breakers topple and reassemble.

At his feet the vagrant weed
dreams between voyages.
The sea-wind scours his eyes as a lone gull
settles to its feast of leavings.

Brushing the sand from his soles he resumes his shoes,
stalking the empty boardwalk, transient as seaweed,
keen as a gull, intrepid, oddly free.
He's weathered the worst.

February winks like a lizard and vanishes,
leaving its tail in his hand.

THE PARTY

They're throwing a party upstairs.
He can hear it carom off the walls and fall
on his sweat-streaked ceiling.

Fretful as a splinter, he'd like
to join the party, senator
from the state of dislocation,
his infinitesimal pressure against history
faint as starlight thrumming the hairs
on a general's wrist.

He ascends from his coldwater grotto,
bobs through the flotsam, fetches up
on a stool by the anchovies.
A mermaid stoops to inquire: *What do
you do?* Her baubles dangle
in the weedy shadow.

I feed on air, he smiles,
*like an orchid. I do
with, my delectable sea-grape.
I do without.*

PASSING GO AGAIN

Across Baltic, in the P.O. parking lot,
the mailmen's Pintos line up at the fence
to watch him pass.
The Grand Old Flag droops on its tall white stalk
like a wilted flower.

By the long green windowless hotels,
swathed against sparrows, the seeded lawns
thrust glass-green spicules through their bandages.
From the schoolyard, tiny bright green screams
pierce morning's shawl.
It's a bad day on Atlantic Avenue
and April's just begun.

Still, it's the only game in town.
A bent black yard-man, raking
dead leaves from the privet, meets the ghost of his smile
with a spectral grin.

While the sun hums overhead to the rustle of money
he scoops up his old bones, and shakes them again.

A HOME AWAY

He comes bearing a cluster of subway posies
or a plaster mermaid
for the wife.

Vagrant, avuncular, perpetual uncle,
rapt nephews bring him ale
in golden cans.

Nieces, flushing, wear his pop-tops
for sweetheart rings.
At Sunday brunch with his old war buddy

our errant templar
nuzzles the dregs like a golden carp,
bottom-feeding in the gene pool.

PILGRIMAGE

Returning to visit the stump
he wonders whether the body politic
still aches in the phantom limb.

It's healed remarkably well.
Where the fruit-man once waxed apples
a laundromat flourishes.

Upstairs in all the fragrant cells
the Puerto Ricans are bearing fruit.

In the steamy bush a macaw screams.

FALL IN THE EQUINOX CAFE

Under the thin, chill, rippling light
of the Miller's High Life sign, his hands
show their true colors as, into the peaceful
sleeves of his windbreaker, the blood
withdraws. He can hear it, softly thrumming
the chambers of his heart.

By the dim gazebo in the park
a maple drains the cool green liquor
from her leaves, and leaves them empty,
revealing aboriginal madders,
ardent reds, parched oranges.

He's thinking of dropping his hands at the feet
of the provident nymph in the vermilion mini,
nursing her second double-bourbon
like a warm brown baby.

PAS DE DEUX

Sunday evening, blinking in the window,
he attends the gingko's shy quadrille with her shadow
on their yard-square, turd-bespangled dancing floor,
watches the amazons strolling their dobermans,
a detachment of semi-detachable widows.
He considers breaking off a piece for himself.

By the relentless heroism of his solitude
almost undone, he anatomizes the enchantments of marriage,
the raptures of coupling, beatitudes of pin and screw,
of latch and chain.

Below, one gilt leaf leaps from the gingko's wrist,
to which it has been clinging since last spring,
twirls and curtseys to the pavement
and hails the first gust travelling west.

SOME NIGHTS

Prodigal brother, my keeper, it's you
who keep our distance, in your frigidaire,
two trays of chill blue bricks
from the unthinkable wall
that prisons whom it would defend.

Faithful as our mère, you keep watch.
Some nights, I know, you rear up in bed
and roar at the mirror.
Your neighbor's long inured,
I can almost hear him slap
the jack of hearts on the widow queen,
playing out his own interminable solitaire.

Some nights I slip one timid pseudopod
through a chink in the distance
between us, prowling the bleak
November beach. I can feel you
fumbling a tatter of seaweed,
popping the seagreen spheres.

Ashiver in the grotto of your nostril,
I catch intimations of mermaids
and elderly carp.

NO NEWS

In the paper tonight it's as he thought. He reads:
The mole has no mating call, although it can make
a couple of sounds that are more or less "conversational."

He contemplates the peacock's wanton scream,
tunes in on the great whale's shameless serenade,
throbbing halfway round the world. A mole of few words,

he plunges through the small talk: *these small sounds*
probably occur when a male and a female mole
stumble into one another. Somewhere, he knows,

a soft grey nymph with moist, myopic eyes
dog-paddles toward him through the fragrant loam.
This moment, the earth might crumble between them,

the last crumbs of topsoil toppling from her velvet nose.

NIGHT FLIGHT

The stewardess leans from the aisle
to tuck him in. His nostrils quail
in a gust of maternal perfume. He murmurs
thankyou to her back.

She'll return with a cart of complimentary
headphones and salty prattle.
The angel of bourbon will press her beautiful thumbs
against his temples.

Dvorak will drip like glucose down the chaste
grey vinyl, to restore them,
seventy breathless celebrants strapped in their pews,
skimming the shingles of oblivion.

The stewardess leans from the aisle

IF PEOPLE HAD ROOTS

When the rivers return to their springs,
when the leaves fly home to their forsaken branches,
when the gypsies go back where they came from,
when the killer revisits the scenes of his innocence,
this eel will wriggle back to his mère
in her seaweed housecoat and shipwreck slippers.
He'll take down his *Almanac of Weeds*
and trace his roots.

Till then he'll persist in his one-man diaspora,
tramping the boondocks with suitcase and six-pack
from wilderness to wilderness,
catching his breath in the villainous cities,
snoring serenely in rented sheets.

If people had roots they'd roost like trees
up to their ankles in earth.
They'd shuck their rags when the north wind called.

METASTASIS

Where is he now? Still drifting,
a cell without a country,
bobbing the arteries of Megalopolis
looking for somewhere harmless to happen.

He passes through airport x-ray portals
like a cosmic particle, passes
roadblocks and customs agents like a gypsy meson,
biding nowhere long.

In a dank hotel in Vera Cruz
he soaks his computer card in sweet white wine,
thoughtfully mutilates a corner,
reloads his empties with lullabies to mermaids
and sends obscene postcards to the editors of *Life*.

DONALD FINKEL was born in New York City and attended public schools there, notably the Bronx High School of Science. He studied sculpture at the Art Students League, and after earning a B.S. in philosophy and an M.A. in English at Columbia left the east for Illinois, Iowa, and finally St. Louis, Mo., where he is Poet in Residence at Washington University. He has lived for several years in Mexico, and travelled widely in the United States. He is married and has three children, three cats, and a Border Collie.

He is the author of *The Clothing's New Emperor* (1959), *Simeon* (1964), *A Joyful Noise* (1966), *Answer Back* (1968), *The Garbage Wars* (1970), *Adequate Earth* (1972), *A Mote in Heaven's Eye* (1975), *Endurance* and *Going Under* (1978) and *What Manner of Beast* (1981). He has been the recipient of a Guggenheim Fellowship and a grant from the National Endowment for the Arts. In 1974 he received the Theodore Roethke Memorial Award for the book-length poem, *Adequate Earth*. In 1980 he received the Morton Dauwen Zabel Award from the Academy and Institute of Arts and Letters for *Endurance* and *Going Under*.